50 Essential Chef's Handbook Recipes

By: Kelly Johnson

Table of Contents

- Classic French Omelette
- Chicken Stock
- Beef Stock
- Vegetable Stock
- Hollandaise Sauce
- Béchamel Sauce
- Velouté Sauce
- Espagnole Sauce
- Tomato Sauce
- Pesto
- Risotto
- Grilled Cheese Sandwich
- Ratatouille
- Beef Wellington
- Coq au Vin
- Beef Bourguignon
- Quiche Lorraine
- Duck Confit
- Caesar Salad
- Vinaigrette
- Beef Tartar
- Lobster Bisque
- Fish Tacos
- Paella
- Bouillabaisse
- Crème Brûlée
- Tiramisu
- Chocolate Soufflé
- Macarons
- Apple Tart Tatin
- Profiteroles
- Baklava
- Sautéed Shrimp Scampi
- Grilled Vegetables
- Chicken Marsala
- Shepherd's Pie

- Sautéed Mushrooms
- Pulled Pork Sandwiches
- Chicken Piccata
- Peking Duck
- Lobster Roll
- Veal Milanese
- Ratatouille Tart
- Pan-Seared Scallops
- Szechuan Chicken
- Shrimp and Grits
- Baked Ziti
- Spanakopita
- Beef Empanadas
- Falafel

Classic French Omelette

Ingredients:

- 3 large eggs
- 1-2 tablespoons unsalted butter
- Salt and freshly ground pepper (to taste)

Instructions:

1. **Prepare the eggs:** Crack the eggs into a bowl, and whisk them gently with a fork or whisk until the yolks and whites are fully combined. Add a pinch of salt and a dash of pepper.

2. **Heat the pan:** Use a non-stick skillet, about 8 inches in diameter. Place the skillet over medium-low heat and add the butter. Let it melt slowly, making sure it coats the bottom and slightly sides of the pan.

3. **Cook the eggs:** Pour the beaten eggs into the pan, swirling them gently so they cover the bottom evenly. As the edges start to set, use a spatula to push them toward the center, letting the uncooked egg flow to the edges. Continue this until most of the eggs are set, but the surface is still slightly runny.

4. **Fold the omelette:** Once the eggs are mostly set but still soft on top, tilt the pan and use a spatula to gently fold one-third of the omelette toward the center. Then fold the opposite third over. You should have a rolled omelette.

5. **Serve:** Carefully slide the omelette onto a plate, seam side down. You can serve it plain or with fresh herbs, cheese, or a filling of your choice.

Chicken Stock

Ingredients:

- 1 whole chicken or 4 lbs chicken bones
- 1 onion, quartered
- 2 carrots, peeled and chopped
- 2 celery stalks, chopped
- 3 garlic cloves, smashed
- 2 bay leaves
- 1 teaspoon black peppercorns
- 10 cups water

Instructions:

1. Place chicken bones and all the vegetables in a large pot.
2. Cover with water and bring to a boil over medium-high heat.
3. Once boiling, reduce heat to low and simmer for 4-6 hours, skimming the surface occasionally.
4. Strain the stock, discarding solids. Cool and store in the fridge or freeze for later use.

Beef Stock

Ingredients:

- 4 lbs beef bones (with marrow)
- 1 onion, quartered
- 2 carrots, peeled and chopped
- 2 celery stalks, chopped
- 4 garlic cloves, smashed
- 2 tablespoons tomato paste
- 1 teaspoon black peppercorns
- 2 bay leaves
- 10 cups water

Instructions:

1. Preheat oven to 400°F (200°C). Roast beef bones on a baking sheet for 30-40 minutes, turning once until browned.
2. Transfer roasted bones to a large pot, add vegetables, and cover with water.
3. Bring to a boil, then reduce to low heat and simmer for 6-8 hours, skimming occasionally.
4. Strain and discard solids. Cool and store.

Vegetable Stock

Ingredients:

- 1 onion, quartered
- 2 carrots, chopped
- 2 celery stalks, chopped
- 1 leek (optional), chopped
- 2 garlic cloves, smashed
- 1 bay leaf
- 1 teaspoon black peppercorns
- 10 cups water

Instructions:

1. Add all vegetables and seasonings to a large pot, cover with water, and bring to a boil.
2. Reduce heat and simmer for 1-2 hours, skimming occasionally.
3. Strain and discard solids. Cool and store.

Hollandaise Sauce

Ingredients:

- 3 egg yolks
- 1 tablespoon lemon juice
- 1 cup unsalted butter, melted
- Salt and white pepper to taste

Instructions:

1. In a double boiler, whisk egg yolks and lemon juice together until pale and slightly thickened.
2. Slowly add melted butter in a thin stream while continuously whisking until the sauce is thick and smooth.
3. Season with salt and white pepper. Serve warm.

Béchamel Sauce

Ingredients:

- 2 tablespoons butter
- 2 tablespoons all-purpose flour
- 2 cups milk
- Salt and nutmeg to taste

Instructions:

1. In a saucepan, melt butter over medium heat. Add flour and whisk for 1-2 minutes to form a roux.
2. Gradually add milk while whisking to prevent lumps. Continue to cook and stir until the sauce thickens.
3. Season with salt and a pinch of nutmeg. Serve.

Velouté Sauce

Ingredients:

- 2 tablespoons butter
- 2 tablespoons all-purpose flour
- 2 cups chicken or fish stock
- Salt and white pepper to taste

Instructions:

1. In a saucepan, melt butter over medium heat. Add flour and cook for 1-2 minutes to create a roux.
2. Gradually add stock while whisking. Continue to cook and stir until the sauce thickens.
3. Season with salt and white pepper. Serve.

Espagnole Sauce (Brown Sauce)

Ingredients:

- 2 tablespoons butter
- 2 tablespoons flour
- 2 cups beef stock
- 1 cup tomatoes, crushed
- 1 onion, chopped
- 1 carrot, chopped
- 1 celery stalk, chopped
- 2 bay leaves
- 1 teaspoon peppercorns

Instructions:

1. In a saucepan, make a brown roux by cooking butter and flour over medium heat until deep brown.
2. Add chopped vegetables and cook for 5 minutes.
3. Gradually add beef stock and tomatoes, whisking continuously.
4. Add bay leaves and peppercorns. Simmer for 45 minutes, then strain.
5. Cool and store.

Tomato Sauce

Ingredients:

- 2 tablespoons olive oil
- 1 onion, chopped
- 2 garlic cloves, minced
- 1 can (28 oz) crushed tomatoes
- 1 teaspoon dried oregano
- 1 teaspoon sugar (optional)
- Salt and pepper to taste

Instructions:

1. Heat olive oil in a pan over medium heat. Add onion and garlic and sauté until softened.
2. Add crushed tomatoes, oregano, and sugar. Simmer for 30 minutes, stirring occasionally.
3. Season with salt and pepper. Serve.

Pesto

Ingredients:

- 2 cups fresh basil leaves
- 1/2 cup pine nuts (or walnuts)
- 2 garlic cloves
- 1/2 cup Parmesan cheese, grated
- 1/2 cup olive oil
- Salt to taste

Instructions:

1. In a food processor, combine basil, pine nuts, garlic, and Parmesan. Pulse until finely chopped.
2. With the processor running, slowly drizzle in olive oil until the pesto reaches a smooth consistency.
3. Season with salt and serve.

Risotto

Ingredients:

- 1 1/2 cups Arborio rice
- 4 cups chicken or vegetable stock (warmed)
- 1 onion, chopped
- 2 tablespoons butter
- 1/2 cup white wine (optional)
- 1 cup Parmesan cheese, grated
- Salt and pepper to taste

Instructions:

1. In a large pan, melt butter over medium heat and sauté onion until softened.
2. Add Arborio rice and cook, stirring, for 1-2 minutes.
3. If using, add white wine and cook until absorbed.
4. Gradually add warmed stock, one ladle at a time, stirring continuously until absorbed before adding more. Continue until the rice is tender and creamy (about 18-20 minutes).
5. Stir in Parmesan cheese and season with salt and pepper. Serve.

Grilled Cheese Sandwich

Ingredients:

- 2 slices of bread
- 2 tablespoons butter, softened
- 2 slices of cheese (American, cheddar, or your choice)

Instructions:

1. Butter one side of each slice of bread.
2. Heat a skillet over medium heat and place one slice of bread, butter side down.
3. Place the cheese slices on the bread and top with the second slice of bread, butter side up.
4. Grill the sandwich until golden brown and crispy on both sides, about 3-4 minutes per side.
5. Serve hot.

Ratatouille

Ingredients:

- 1 eggplant, diced
- 1 zucchini, diced
- 1 bell pepper, diced
- 1 onion, diced
- 3 tomatoes, chopped
- 2 garlic cloves, minced
- 2 tablespoons olive oil
- 1 tablespoon fresh thyme
- Salt and pepper to taste

Instructions:

1. Heat olive oil in a large pan over medium heat. Add onion and garlic and sauté until soft.
2. Add eggplant, zucchini, bell pepper, and cook for 5-7 minutes.
3. Add tomatoes, thyme, salt, and pepper. Simmer for 20-25 minutes until vegetables are tender.
4. Serve warm as a side dish.

Beef Wellington

Ingredients:

- 2 lb beef tenderloin (center-cut)
- 2 tablespoons olive oil
- 2 tablespoons Dijon mustard
- 1/2 lb mushrooms, finely chopped
- 2 tablespoons butter
- 1/4 cup dry white wine
- 1 sheet puff pastry
- 1 egg (for egg wash)
- Salt and pepper

Instructions:

1. Preheat oven to 400°F (200°C). Sear beef tenderloin in olive oil in a hot pan until browned on all sides. Remove from heat and brush with mustard.
2. Cook mushrooms in butter until soft, then add wine and cook until dry.
3. Roll out puff pastry and place mushrooms on the center. Place the beef on top and wrap it with the pastry.
4. Brush the pastry with egg wash and bake for 35-40 minutes or until golden brown. Let rest before serving.

Coq au Vin

Ingredients:

- 4 chicken thighs
- 1 bottle red wine
- 2 cups chicken stock
- 2 tablespoons olive oil
- 1 onion, chopped
- 2 carrots, chopped
- 2 garlic cloves, minced
- 1 cup mushrooms, sliced
- 2 tablespoons flour
- 2 teaspoons fresh thyme
- Salt and pepper

Instructions:

1. Heat olive oil in a large pot. Brown chicken thighs on both sides and set aside.
2. In the same pot, sauté onion, carrots, garlic, and mushrooms until softened.
3. Add flour and cook for 1 minute, then add wine and chicken stock. Bring to a simmer.
4. Return chicken to the pot, add thyme, salt, and pepper, and simmer for 1-1.5 hours.
5. Serve with mashed potatoes or crusty bread.

Beef Bourguignon

Ingredients:

- 2 lb beef chuck, cut into cubes
- 1 bottle red wine
- 2 cups beef stock
- 2 tablespoons olive oil
- 1 onion, chopped
- 2 carrots, chopped
- 3 garlic cloves, minced
- 2 tablespoons tomato paste
- 1 bouquet garni (thyme, rosemary, and bay leaf)
- 1 cup pearl onions
- 1/2 lb mushrooms, sliced
- Salt and pepper

Instructions:

1. Brown beef cubes in olive oil in a large pot. Remove and set aside.
2. In the same pot, sauté onion, carrots, and garlic. Add tomato paste and cook for 2 minutes.
3. Add wine, beef stock, and bouquet garni. Return beef to the pot and simmer for 2-3 hours until tender.
4. In a separate pan, sauté pearl onions and mushrooms. Add to the stew and simmer for another 30 minutes.
5. Serve with mashed potatoes or crusty bread.

Quiche Lorraine

Ingredients:

- 1 pie crust (store-bought or homemade)
- 6 large eggs
- 1 cup heavy cream
- 1 cup grated Gruyère cheese
- 1/2 lb cooked bacon, crumbled
- Salt and pepper to taste

Instructions:

1. Preheat oven to 375°F (190°C). Bake the pie crust for 10 minutes to set.
2. Whisk eggs, heavy cream, cheese, and bacon together. Season with salt and pepper.
3. Pour mixture into the partially baked pie crust and bake for 30-35 minutes until set.
4. Let cool slightly before slicing. Serve warm.

Duck Confit

Ingredients:

- 4 duck legs
- 4 cups duck fat (or enough to cover duck legs)
- 3 garlic cloves, smashed
- 2 sprigs fresh thyme
- Salt and pepper

Instructions:

1. Preheat oven to 250°F (120°C). Season duck legs with salt and pepper.
2. Place duck legs in a baking dish and cover with duck fat. Add garlic and thyme.
3. Slow-cook in the oven for 2-3 hours until tender.
4. To crisp the skin, heat a skillet and sear the duck legs, skin-side down, until crispy.
5. Serve with roasted potatoes or salad.

Caesar Salad

Ingredients:

- 1 head romaine lettuce, chopped
- 1/4 cup grated Parmesan cheese
- 1 cup croutons
- 1/4 cup Caesar dressing (store-bought or homemade)

Instructions:

1. Toss chopped lettuce with Caesar dressing until evenly coated.
2. Sprinkle with Parmesan cheese and croutons.
3. Serve immediately.

Vinaigrette

Ingredients:

- 3 tablespoons olive oil
- 1 tablespoon red wine vinegar
- 1 teaspoon Dijon mustard
- Salt and pepper to taste

Instructions:

1. Whisk all ingredients together until emulsified.
2. Adjust seasoning to taste. Serve over salads.

Beef Tartare

Ingredients:

- 1/2 lb beef tenderloin, finely chopped
- 1 egg yolk
- 2 tablespoons capers, chopped
- 1 tablespoon Dijon mustard
- 1 tablespoon Worcestershire sauce
- Salt and pepper to taste
- Chopped parsley for garnish

Instructions:

1. Mix the beef, egg yolk, capers, mustard, Worcestershire sauce, salt, and pepper in a bowl.
2. Shape into a patty or serve in a bowl.
3. Garnish with chopped parsley and serve with toasted bread or crackers.

Lobster Bisque

Ingredients:

- 2 lobster tails, cooked and chopped
- 4 cups seafood stock
- 1/2 cup dry white wine
- 1/4 cup butter
- 1/2 cup onion, chopped
- 2 garlic cloves, minced
- 1/2 cup tomato paste
- 1 teaspoon paprika
- 1/2 cup heavy cream
- Salt and pepper to taste
- Fresh parsley for garnish

Instructions:

1. In a large pot, melt butter and sauté onion and garlic until softened.
2. Add tomato paste and paprika, cooking for 2 minutes.
3. Pour in wine and seafood stock, bring to a boil, then reduce heat and simmer for 15-20 minutes.
4. Add lobster meat and heavy cream, and simmer for another 5 minutes.
5. Use an immersion blender to puree the bisque until smooth.
6. Season with salt and pepper and garnish with parsley. Serve warm.

Fish Tacos

Ingredients:

- 1 lb white fish fillets (like cod or tilapia)
- 1 tablespoon olive oil
- 1 teaspoon cumin
- 1 teaspoon chili powder
- Salt and pepper to taste
- 8 small corn tortillas
- 1 cup shredded cabbage
- 1/2 cup salsa
- 1/4 cup sour cream
- Lime wedges for serving

Instructions:

1. Season the fish with olive oil, cumin, chili powder, salt, and pepper.
2. Heat a skillet over medium heat and cook fish for 3-4 minutes per side, until flaky.
3. Warm tortillas in a dry pan or microwave.
4. Flake the fish and place in tortillas. Top with shredded cabbage, salsa, and sour cream.
5. Serve with lime wedges.

Paella

Ingredients:

- 1/4 cup olive oil
- 1 onion, chopped
- 1 bell pepper, chopped
- 2 garlic cloves, minced
- 1 1/2 cups Arborio rice
- 1/4 teaspoon saffron threads
- 4 cups chicken or seafood stock
- 1 lb mixed seafood (shrimp, mussels, clams)
- 1/2 lb chicken thighs, cooked and chopped
- 1/2 cup peas
- Salt and pepper to taste
- Lemon wedges for serving

Instructions:

1. Heat olive oil in a large pan over medium heat. Sauté onion, bell pepper, and garlic until softened.
2. Add rice and saffron, stirring to coat the rice in oil.
3. Gradually add stock, stirring until absorbed. Add seafood, chicken, and peas, and cook for 10-15 minutes.
4. Season with salt and pepper and serve with lemon wedges.

Bouillabaisse

Ingredients:

- 1/4 cup olive oil
- 1 onion, chopped
- 2 leeks, chopped
- 2 celery stalks, chopped
- 2 garlic cloves, minced
- 2 tomatoes, chopped
- 1/2 teaspoon saffron threads
- 1 1/2 lb mixed seafood (white fish, shrimp, mussels, clams)
- 4 cups fish stock
- 1/2 cup dry white wine
- 1 tablespoon tomato paste
- Salt and pepper to taste
- Fresh parsley for garnish

Instructions:

1. Heat olive oil in a large pot over medium heat. Add onion, leeks, celery, and garlic, sautéing until softened.
2. Add tomatoes, saffron, fish stock, white wine, and tomato paste. Bring to a simmer and cook for 10 minutes.
3. Add seafood and cook for another 10 minutes until the fish is cooked through.
4. Season with salt and pepper, and garnish with fresh parsley before serving.

Crème Brûlée

Ingredients:

- 2 cups heavy cream
- 1 vanilla bean or 1 tablespoon vanilla extract
- 5 large egg yolks
- 1/2 cup sugar
- 1/4 cup brown sugar (for topping)

Instructions:

1. Preheat oven to 325°F (163°C). Heat cream and vanilla in a saucepan until it simmers. Remove from heat.
2. Whisk egg yolks and sugar until smooth. Gradually add hot cream to the egg mixture while whisking.
3. Pour mixture into ramekins and place in a baking dish. Fill the dish with hot water halfway up the sides of the ramekins.
4. Bake for 45 minutes or until set. Cool, then refrigerate for at least 2 hours.
5. Before serving, sprinkle brown sugar on top and caramelize with a kitchen torch.

Tiramisu

Ingredients:

- 1 1/2 cups strong coffee, cooled
- 1/4 cup rum or Marsala wine
- 6 large egg yolks
- 3/4 cup sugar
- 1 1/2 cups mascarpone cheese
- 1 1/2 cups heavy cream
- 1 package ladyfingers
- Cocoa powder for dusting

Instructions:

1. Mix coffee and rum in a shallow dish. Quickly dip ladyfingers into the coffee mixture and layer them in a baking dish.
2. In a bowl, whisk egg yolks and sugar until thick and pale. Add mascarpone cheese and mix until smooth.
3. In another bowl, whip heavy cream until stiff peaks form. Fold into the mascarpone mixture.
4. Layer the mascarpone mixture over the ladyfingers. Repeat the layers.
5. Refrigerate for at least 4 hours, then dust with cocoa powder before serving.

Chocolate Soufflé

Ingredients:

- 1/2 cup heavy cream
- 6 oz dark chocolate, chopped
- 3 large egg yolks
- 3 large egg whites
- 1/4 cup sugar
- 1 tablespoon butter (for greasing)

Instructions:

1. Preheat oven to 375°F (190°C). Butter and sugar individual ramekins.
2. Heat cream in a saucepan and pour over the chopped chocolate. Stir until smooth.
3. Whisk egg yolks into the chocolate mixture. Set aside.
4. Beat egg whites until soft peaks form. Gradually add sugar and beat until stiff peaks form.
5. Gently fold egg whites into the chocolate mixture. Pour into ramekins and bake for 12-15 minutes until puffed.
6. Serve immediately.

Macarons

Ingredients:

- 1 1/2 cups powdered sugar
- 1 cup almond flour
- 3 large egg whites
- 1/4 cup sugar
- Filling (buttercream, ganache, or jam)

Instructions:

1. Preheat oven to 325°F (163°C). Line baking sheets with parchment paper.
2. Sift powdered sugar and almond flour together. Set aside.
3. Beat egg whites until soft peaks form, then gradually add sugar and beat until stiff peaks form.
4. Fold in almond flour mixture, then pipe onto baking sheets into small rounds.
5. Bake for 10-12 minutes, then let cool.
6. Fill with your choice of filling and sandwich together.

Apple Tart Tatin

Ingredients:

- 6-8 apples, peeled, cored, and halved
- 1/2 cup unsalted butter
- 1 cup sugar
- 1 sheet puff pastry
- Whipped cream for serving

Instructions:

1. Preheat oven to 375°F (190°C).
2. In a skillet, melt butter and sugar over medium heat until caramelized. Add apples and cook for 10-15 minutes.
3. Cover apples with puff pastry and bake for 25-30 minutes.
4. Invert onto a plate and serve with whipped cream.

Profiteroles

Ingredients:

- 1 cup water
- 1/2 cup butter
- 1 cup all-purpose flour
- 4 large eggs
- 1 cup whipped cream (for filling)
- Chocolate sauce (for topping)

Instructions:

1. Preheat oven to 400°F (200°C). In a saucepan, combine water and butter, bringing to a boil.
2. Stir in flour until a dough forms. Remove from heat and cool slightly.
3. Beat in eggs one at a time until smooth.
4. Pipe dough into small mounds on a baking sheet and bake for 20-25 minutes.
5. Fill with whipped cream and top with chocolate sauce.

Baklava

Ingredients:

- 1 package phyllo dough
- 2 cups mixed nuts (pistachios, walnuts, almonds)
- 1 teaspoon cinnamon
- 1 cup honey
- 1/2 cup sugar
- 1/2 cup water
- 1 tablespoon lemon juice
- 1 cup butter, melted

Instructions:

1. Preheat oven to 350°F (175°C). Chop nuts and mix with cinnamon.
2. Brush a baking dish with butter and layer phyllo dough, brushing each sheet with butter.
3. Sprinkle a layer of nut mixture, then top with more phyllo. Repeat until all filling is used.
4. Cut the baklava into squares and bake for 45 minutes.
5. In a saucepan, combine honey, sugar, water, and lemon juice. Bring to a boil and simmer for 10 minutes.
6. Pour syrup over baked baklava and let it cool before serving.

Sautéed Shrimp Scampi

Ingredients:

- 1 lb large shrimp, peeled and deveined
- 4 tablespoons butter
- 4 garlic cloves, minced
- 1/2 teaspoon red pepper flakes (optional)
- 1/2 cup dry white wine
- 1 lemon, juiced
- 1/4 cup chopped parsley
- Salt and pepper to taste
- 8 oz pasta (linguine or spaghetti)

Instructions:

1. Cook pasta according to package instructions, then drain and set aside.
2. In a large skillet, melt butter over medium heat. Add garlic and red pepper flakes, cooking until fragrant, about 1 minute.
3. Add shrimp to the skillet, season with salt and pepper, and cook for 2-3 minutes per side until pink and opaque.
4. Pour in wine and lemon juice, simmer for 2 minutes to reduce slightly.
5. Toss the cooked pasta in the skillet, coating it with the sauce.
6. Sprinkle with chopped parsley and serve immediately.

Grilled Vegetables

Ingredients:

- 1 zucchini, sliced
- 1 bell pepper, cut into chunks
- 1 red onion, sliced
- 1 cup cherry tomatoes
- 2 tablespoons olive oil
- 1 teaspoon dried oregano
- Salt and pepper to taste

Instructions:

1. Preheat the grill to medium heat.
2. Toss the vegetables with olive oil, oregano, salt, and pepper.
3. Grill the vegetables for 4-5 minutes per side, until tender and charred.
4. Serve warm as a side dish.

Chicken Marsala

Ingredients:

- 4 boneless, skinless chicken breasts
- 1/4 cup flour
- 2 tablespoons olive oil
- 1 cup Marsala wine
- 1 cup chicken stock
- 8 oz mushrooms, sliced
- 2 tablespoons butter
- Salt and pepper to taste

Instructions:

1. Lightly dredge the chicken breasts in flour, seasoning with salt and pepper.
2. Heat olive oil in a skillet over medium-high heat. Brown chicken on both sides, then remove from the pan.
3. Add mushrooms to the pan and sauté for 3-4 minutes.
4. Pour in the Marsala wine and chicken stock, scraping up any browned bits from the pan. Simmer for 10 minutes to reduce the sauce.
5. Return chicken to the pan and cook for another 5-7 minutes until the chicken is cooked through.
6. Stir in butter and serve.

Shepherd's Pie

Ingredients:

- 1 lb ground beef or lamb
- 1 onion, chopped
- 2 carrots, diced
- 1 cup peas
- 2 tablespoons tomato paste
- 1 cup beef broth
- 2 tablespoons Worcestershire sauce
- 4 large potatoes, peeled and boiled
- 1/4 cup milk
- 2 tablespoons butter
- Salt and pepper to taste

Instructions:

1. Preheat oven to 375°F (190°C).
2. In a pan, brown the ground beef or lamb with the onion. Add carrots and cook for 5 minutes.
3. Stir in tomato paste, beef broth, Worcestershire sauce, and peas. Simmer until thickened, about 10 minutes.
4. Mash the boiled potatoes with milk, butter, salt, and pepper until smooth.
5. Transfer the meat mixture to a baking dish, then top with mashed potatoes.
6. Bake for 25-30 minutes until the top is golden brown.

Sautéed Mushrooms

Ingredients:

- 1 lb mushrooms, sliced
- 2 tablespoons olive oil
- 2 garlic cloves, minced
- 1 tablespoon fresh thyme, chopped
- Salt and pepper to taste

Instructions:

1. Heat olive oil in a skillet over medium heat.
2. Add mushrooms and sauté for 5-7 minutes until browned and tender.
3. Stir in garlic and thyme, cooking for another minute.
4. Season with salt and pepper, then serve warm.

Pulled Pork Sandwiches

Ingredients:

- 2 lbs pork shoulder
- 1 tablespoon olive oil
- 1 onion, chopped
- 2 garlic cloves, minced
- 1 cup barbecue sauce
- 1/2 cup apple cider vinegar
- 1/2 teaspoon smoked paprika
- Salt and pepper to taste
- 4 sandwich buns

Instructions:

1. Preheat the oven to 300°F (150°C).
2. Rub the pork shoulder with olive oil, smoked paprika, salt, and pepper.
3. Sear the pork in a hot pan until browned on all sides.
4. Transfer the pork to a roasting pan, add onion, garlic, barbecue sauce, and apple cider vinegar. Cover and roast for 3-4 hours until tender.
5. Shred the pork with a fork and serve on buns with extra barbecue sauce.

Chicken Piccata

Ingredients:

- 4 boneless, skinless chicken breasts
- 1/4 cup flour
- 2 tablespoons olive oil
- 1/4 cup white wine
- 1/4 cup lemon juice
- 1/4 cup capers
- 2 tablespoons butter
- Salt and pepper to taste

Instructions:

1. Lightly dredge the chicken breasts in flour, seasoning with salt and pepper.
2. Heat olive oil in a pan over medium-high heat. Cook the chicken for 3-4 minutes per side until golden and cooked through. Remove from the pan.
3. Add white wine, lemon juice, and capers to the pan, scraping up any browned bits.
4. Simmer for 3-4 minutes, then stir in butter to create a sauce.
5. Return chicken to the pan, spoon sauce over the top, and serve.

Peking Duck

Ingredients:

- 1 whole duck (about 5 lbs)
- 1/4 cup soy sauce
- 2 tablespoons honey
- 2 tablespoons rice vinegar
- 1 tablespoon five-spice powder
- 1 tablespoon grated ginger
- 2 tablespoons sugar
- 4-6 scallions
- 12-16 thin pancakes or tortillas

Instructions:

1. Preheat oven to 375°F (190°C). Score the duck skin and rub with five-spice powder, soy sauce, honey, vinegar, ginger, and sugar.
2. Roast the duck for 1.5-2 hours, basting every 30 minutes.
3. Once the skin is crispy and golden, let the duck rest for 10 minutes before carving.
4. Serve with scallions, pancakes, and hoisin sauce.

Lobster Roll

Ingredients:

- 2 cooked lobster tails, chopped
- 1/4 cup mayonnaise
- 1 tablespoon lemon juice
- 1 tablespoon chopped fresh parsley
- 2 rolls (preferably New England-style)
- Butter for toasting buns
- Salt and pepper to taste

Instructions:

1. In a bowl, mix lobster, mayonnaise, lemon juice, parsley, salt, and pepper.
2. Butter the rolls and toast them in a pan until golden brown.
3. Fill the rolls with lobster mixture and serve.

Veal Milanese

Ingredients:

- 4 veal cutlets
- 1 cup flour
- 2 large eggs, beaten
- 1 cup breadcrumbs
- 1/4 cup Parmesan cheese
- 1/4 cup olive oil
- Salt and pepper to taste
- Lemon wedges for serving

Instructions:

1. Season veal cutlets with salt and pepper. Dredge in flour, dip in beaten eggs, and coat in breadcrumbs mixed with Parmesan.
2. Heat olive oil in a large skillet over medium heat. Fry veal cutlets for 3-4 minutes per side until golden brown and crispy.
3. Serve with lemon wedges.

Ratatouille Tart

Ingredients:

- 1 sheet puff pastry
- 1 zucchini, sliced
- 1 eggplant, sliced
- 1 bell pepper, sliced
- 1 tomato, sliced
- 2 tablespoons olive oil
- 1 teaspoon dried herbs (thyme, oregano)
- Salt and pepper to taste

Instructions:

1. Preheat oven to 375°F (190°C).
2. Roll out puff pastry on a baking sheet and prick with a fork.
3. Arrange sliced vegetables on top of the pastry, overlapping in rows.
4. Drizzle with olive oil, sprinkle with dried herbs, salt, and pepper.
5. Bake for 25-30 minutes until the pastry is golden and the vegetables are tender.

Pan-Seared Scallops

Ingredients:

- 1 lb large sea scallops
- 2 tablespoons olive oil
- 2 tablespoons butter
- 2 garlic cloves, minced
- 1 tablespoon fresh lemon juice
- Salt and pepper to taste
- Fresh parsley, chopped for garnish

Instructions:

1. Pat the scallops dry with paper towels and season with salt and pepper.
2. Heat olive oil in a large skillet over medium-high heat.
3. Add the scallops and cook for 2-3 minutes per side, until a golden crust forms. Do not overcrowd the pan.
4. Add butter and garlic to the skillet, and cook for another minute.
5. Remove from heat, drizzle with lemon juice, and garnish with fresh parsley. Serve immediately.

Szechuan Chicken

Ingredients:

- 1 lb chicken breasts, cut into bite-sized pieces
- 2 tablespoons soy sauce
- 2 tablespoons cornstarch
- 2 tablespoons vegetable oil
- 1 onion, chopped
- 2 bell peppers, sliced
- 3 garlic cloves, minced
- 1 tablespoon ginger, minced
- 2 tablespoons Szechuan peppercorns
- 3 tablespoons soy sauce
- 2 tablespoons rice vinegar
- 1 tablespoon hoisin sauce
- 1 tablespoon chili paste
- 1/2 cup water

Instructions:

1. In a bowl, toss the chicken pieces with 2 tablespoons soy sauce and cornstarch to coat.
2. Heat vegetable oil in a large pan over medium-high heat. Add chicken and cook until browned, about 5-7 minutes. Remove and set aside.
3. In the same pan, add onion, bell peppers, garlic, and ginger. Stir-fry for 3-4 minutes.
4. Add Szechuan peppercorns, soy sauce, rice vinegar, hoisin sauce, chili paste, and water. Stir to combine.
5. Return chicken to the pan and cook for another 3-5 minutes until the sauce thickens and the chicken is coated.
6. Serve hot over rice.

Shrimp and Grits

Ingredients:

- 1 lb shrimp, peeled and deveined
- 1 cup grits (stone-ground preferred)
- 4 cups water or chicken stock
- 2 tablespoons butter
- 1 cup cheddar cheese, grated
- 1/2 teaspoon garlic powder
- 1 tablespoon olive oil
- 4 bacon slices, chopped
- 2 garlic cloves, minced
- 1 tablespoon lemon juice
- Salt and pepper to taste
- Fresh parsley for garnish

Instructions:

1. Bring water or stock to a boil in a medium pot. Stir in grits, reduce heat to low, and cook for 20-25 minutes, stirring occasionally until thickened.
2. Stir in butter, cheese, garlic powder, salt, and pepper. Keep warm.
3. In a skillet, cook bacon over medium heat until crispy. Remove and set aside.
4. In the same skillet, heat olive oil over medium heat. Add garlic and cook for 1 minute.
5. Add shrimp to the skillet and cook for 2-3 minutes per side, until pink and cooked through. Drizzle with lemon juice and season with salt and pepper.
6. To serve, spoon grits into bowls, top with shrimp, sprinkle with bacon, and garnish with fresh parsley.

Baked Ziti

Ingredients:

- 1 lb ziti pasta
- 3 cups marinara sauce
- 15 oz ricotta cheese
- 2 cups shredded mozzarella cheese
- 1/2 cup grated Parmesan cheese
- 1 egg
- 2 teaspoons dried basil
- 1 teaspoon dried oregano
- 1/2 teaspoon garlic powder
- Salt and pepper to taste
- Fresh basil for garnish

Instructions:

1. Preheat oven to 375°F (190°C). Cook ziti pasta according to package directions, drain, and set aside.
2. In a large bowl, mix ricotta, mozzarella, Parmesan, egg, basil, oregano, garlic powder, salt, and pepper.
3. In a baking dish, spread a thin layer of marinara sauce. Add half of the cooked ziti, followed by half of the cheese mixture. Repeat layers with remaining pasta and cheese mixture.
4. Top with remaining marinara sauce and mozzarella cheese.
5. Cover with foil and bake for 25 minutes. Remove foil and bake for an additional 10 minutes, until bubbly and golden.
6. Garnish with fresh basil and serve.

Spanakopita

Ingredients:

- 1 lb spinach, fresh or frozen (thawed and drained)
- 1/2 lb feta cheese, crumbled
- 1/4 cup ricotta cheese
- 1 onion, finely chopped
- 2 cloves garlic, minced
- 1 tablespoon olive oil
- 2 eggs, beaten
- 1/4 teaspoon nutmeg
- 1 package phyllo dough
- 1/4 cup butter, melted
- Salt and pepper to taste

Instructions:

1. Preheat oven to 375°F (190°C). Heat olive oil in a pan over medium heat and sauté onion and garlic until softened.
2. Add spinach, cook for 2-3 minutes, then remove from heat and let cool. Drain any excess moisture.
3. In a bowl, mix spinach, feta, ricotta, eggs, nutmeg, salt, and pepper.
4. Brush a baking dish with melted butter and layer 3-4 sheets of phyllo dough, brushing each with butter.
5. Add spinach filling and top with 3-4 more sheets of phyllo dough. Brush each layer with butter.
6. Fold in the edges of the phyllo and bake for 35-40 minutes until golden brown.
7. Let cool for a few minutes before serving.

Beef Empanadas

Ingredients:

- 1 lb ground beef
- 1 onion, finely chopped
- 2 cloves garlic, minced
- 1/4 cup green olives, chopped
- 1/4 cup raisins (optional)
- 1 teaspoon cumin
- 1/2 teaspoon paprika
- 1/4 teaspoon chili powder
- Salt and pepper to taste
- 1 package empanada dough discs
- 1 egg, beaten (for egg wash)
- Vegetable oil for frying

Instructions:

1. Heat oil in a pan over medium heat. Cook ground beef with onion and garlic until browned.
2. Add olives, raisins, cumin, paprika, chili powder, salt, and pepper. Cook for another 5 minutes until the mixture is well combined.
3. Let the filling cool slightly. Place a spoonful of the filling in the center of each empanada dough disc.
4. Fold the dough over the filling and press the edges to seal. Crimp the edges with a fork.
5. Brush with beaten egg and fry in hot oil for 3-4 minutes per side until golden brown.
6. Drain on paper towels and serve warm.

Falafel

Ingredients:

- 1 cup dried chickpeas
- 1 onion, chopped
- 2 garlic cloves, minced
- 1/4 cup fresh parsley, chopped
- 1/4 cup fresh cilantro, chopped
- 1 teaspoon cumin
- 1 teaspoon coriander
- Salt and pepper to taste
- 1 teaspoon baking powder
- 4-6 tablespoons flour
- Vegetable oil for frying

Instructions:

1. Soak chickpeas in water overnight. Drain and rinse.
2. In a food processor, pulse chickpeas, onion, garlic, parsley, cilantro, cumin, coriander, salt, and pepper until smooth but not pureed.
3. Add baking powder and flour, then process until the mixture holds together when squeezed. If too wet, add more flour.
4. Shape the mixture into small balls or patties.
5. Heat oil in a pan over medium-high heat and fry the falafel for 3-4 minutes per side until golden brown.
6. Drain on paper towels and serve with tahini sauce or in pita bread with salad.

www.ingramcontent.com/pod-product-compliance
Lightning Source LLC
LaVergne TN
LVHW081336060526
838201LV00055B/2684